DOMINOES

The Sorcerer's Apprentice

QUICK STARTER | 250 HEADWORDS

OXFORD

UNIVERSITY PRESS

Great Clarendon Street, Oxford, OX2 6DP, United Kingdom

Oxford University Press is a department of the University of Oxford.
It furthers the University's objective of excellence in research, scholarship,
and education by publishing worldwide. Oxford is a registered trade
mark of Oxford University Press in the UK and in certain other countries

© Oxford University Press 2013

The moral rights of the author have been asserted

First published in Dominoes 2013

2017 2016 2015 2014 2013

10 9 8 7 6 5 4 3 2 1

No unauthorized photocopying

Links to third party websites are provided by Oxford in good faith and
for information only. Oxford disclaims any responsibility for the materials
contained in any third party website referenced in this work

ISBN: 978 0 19 424976 8   Book
ISBN: 978 0 19 424993 5   Book and MultiROM Pack
MultiROM not available separately

Printed in China

This book is printed on paper from certified and well-managed sources

ACKNOWLEDGEMENTS

Cover artwork and illustrations by: Kanako Damerum and Yuzuru Takasaki

The series editors wish to express their thanks to Stephanie Tural for her helpful comments on the story.

The publisher would like to thank the following for permission to reproduce photographs: Alamy
Images p.27 (Fantasia/AF archive); Corbis p.27 (Portrait of Lucian of Samosata/Michael
Nicholson); Getty Images p.24 (Snow covered Japanese garden/Bruce Forster); Kobal
Collection p.27 (*The Sorcerer's Apprentice*/Walt Disney Pictures); Rex Features p.26 (Johann
Wolfgang Von Goethe statue/Action Press).

DOMINOES

Series Editors: Bill Bowler and Sue Parminter

The Sorcerer's Apprentice

Retold by Bill Bowler

Illustrated by Kanako Damerum and Yuzuru Takasaki

Bill Bowler studied English Literature at Cambridge University and mime in Paris before he became an English language teacher, trainer, and materials writer. He loves the theatre, cinema, history, art – and travelling. He also enjoys reading books and writing poetry in his free time. Bill lives in Alicante with his wife, Sue Parminter, and their three children. This Dominoes retelling of *The Sorcerer's Apprentice* is based on earlier versions, but set in Japan – a country that Bill has visited and finds fascinating.

OXFORD
UNIVERSITY PRESS

Story Characters

Yukio

Mariko

Kunio

The sorcerer

Contents

BEFORE READING

The sorcerer's apprentice, Yukio, is a boy from old Japan. What do you think happens in his story? Match each picture with a gapped sentence.

1

Yukio

2

the sorcerer

a Yukio lives happily in the country with… ☐.

b … ☐ lives not far away from them.

3

Mariko

4

Kunio

c Kunio doesn't understand… ☐.

d Mariko and Kunio meet in the… ☐.

e Mariko and Kunio marry in the… ☐.

5

spring

6

summer

f Yukio leaves for the town in the… ☐.

g Yukio wants to learn from… ☐.

7

fall

8

winter

h Yukio begins learning from his new teacher in the… ☐.

Yukio lives in a little village. It is in the country, not far from Kyoto – in old Japan.

Yukio's **parents** are dead. So he lives with his older sister, Mariko. They live in the old family house.

Mariko works **hard** in the garden, and the house. Yukio helps her. For some years they are happy **together**.

parents mother and father

hard a lot, strongly

together with someone or near to someone

1

But then Kunio arrives. Kunio lives on a **farm** near their house. He is a farmer.

One **spring** day, Kunio is walking past their house. Suddenly he sees Mariko. She is standing under the **cherry** tree in her garden. It has beautiful **blossoms** on it.

Kunio smiles at Mariko, and Mariko smiles at Kunio. But Yukio does not smile. He does not like Kunio.

farm a house with land in the country

spring the warm time of the year when the first flowers arrive

cherry (*plural* **cherries**) a little, round, red fruit that has a hard stone in the middle

blossom a flower on a tree in spring time

READING CHECK

Are these sentences true or false? Tick the boxes.

		True	False
a	Yukio lives in a village not far from Tokyo.	☐	☑
b	Yukio's mother and father are dead.	☐	☐
c	Yukio is Mariko's older brother.	☐	☐
d	Mariko and Yukio live in an old house.	☐	☐
e	Kunio is a teacher.	☐	☐
f	Kunio lives near Mariko and Yukio's house.	☐	☐
g	Kunio first sees Mariko in the spring.	☐	☐
h	Mariko is standing under an apple tree.	☐	☐
i	Yukio likes Kunio.	☐	☐

GUESS WHAT

What happens in the next chapter? Tick the boxes.

a Yukio …
   1 ☐ goes and lives on Kunio's farm with Mariko.
   2 ☐ works hard for Kunio.

b Mariko …
   1 ☐ talks and laughs with Kunio.
   2 ☐ speaks angrily to Yukio.

c Kunio …
   1 ☐ understands Yukio very well.
   2 ☐ works hard on his farm from morning to night.

Chapter 2

On Kunio's farm

After that, Kunio often visits Mariko. They talk and laugh together. Sometimes Kunio drinks **tea** with Mariko and her brother. Yukio never speaks to Kunio when he visits.

One **summer** evening, Mariko and Kunio are watching the **fireflies** in the garden. Kunio tells Mariko, 'I want to **marry** you. Do you want to marry me?' 'I do,' she answers him happily.

tea a drink that you make when you put plant leaves in very hot water

summer the hot time of the year; it comes after spring

firefly small animal with six legs that flies at night and gives light from its body

marry to make someone your husband or wife

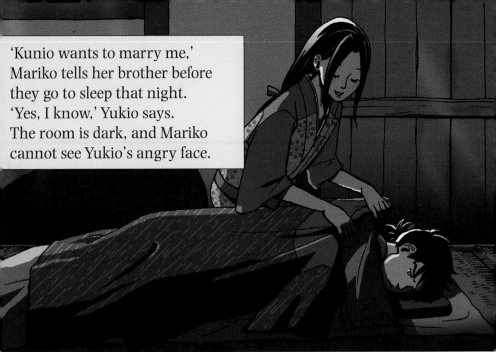

'Kunio wants to marry me,' Mariko tells her brother before they go to sleep that night. 'Yes, I know,' Yukio says. The room is dark, and Mariko cannot see Yukio's angry face.

So Mariko marries Kunio. After that, she goes and lives in Kunio's house. She takes Yukio with her.

Kunio works on the farm from morning to night.

Yukio doesn't work. He likes looking up at the hills and the sky. He likes talking to the **birds**, and sleeping under the trees.

Kunio cannot understand Yukio. 'Your young brother doesn't help me on the farm,' he tells his **wife**. 'What's the matter with him?' 'I don't know,' Mariko answers. '**Maybe** he isn't interested in farm work. Maybe he wants to do a different **job**.' 'Then maybe he must leave the farm and look for work,' Kunio says.

bird an animal that can fly through the sky

wife a woman living with a man

maybe perhaps

job work

READING CHECK

Choose the correct words to complete these sentences.

a Kunio and Mariko often talk and *cry* / *laugh* together.

b Kunio sometimes drinks *tea* / *milk* with Mariko and Yukio.

c One summer evening, Kunio and Mariko watch *cats* / *fireflies*.

d Kunio wants to *marry* / *leave* Mariko.

e Yukio is *excited* / *angry* when Mariko tells him about Kunio.

f Mariko marries *Kunio* / *the sorcerer* soon after that.

g Mariko takes *Yukio* / *her cat* with her to Kunio's house.

h Yukio *works* / *doesn't work* a lot on Kunio's farm.

i Kunio *understands* / *doesn't understand* Yukio.

GUESS WHAT

What happens in the next chapter? Tick three sentences.

a Yukio begins working hard on Kunio's farm. ☐

b Yukio goes and lives in his parents' old house again. ☐

c Yukio goes and looks for work in the town. ☐

d Mariko cries when her brother leaves home. ☐

e Kunio goes with Yukio to the town. ☐

f Mariko goes with Yukio to the town. ☐

g Yukio finds a job in the town. ☐

Chapter 3 Looking for work

Soon the **fall** arrives. The green **leaves** on the trees change to yellow and red. Kunio wants to **sell** things from his farm in the nearest town. He takes Yukio with him.

'Goodbye,' Mariko says when they are leaving. 'Come back soon.' 'Yes, Mariko,' Kunio says, and he smiles. 'Goodbye, sister,' Yukio cries. 'Thanks for everything.'

On the road, Kunio speaks to Yukio. 'Maybe you can find a job today,' he says. 'Yes, maybe I can,' the boy answers.

fall the time of the year after the summer

sell to take money for something

leaf (*plural* **leaves**) we find these flat, usually green things, on trees and plants

When they arrive in the town, Kunio sells everything from his **cart**. He soon has a lot of money.

Yukio walks through the town. He is interested in everything there.

Suddenly he sees an interesting old man. He is wearing black **clothes**. 'Are you looking for work?' the old man asks. 'I am,' Yukio answers. 'But what's your job?' 'I'm a **sorcerer**,' the old man smiles. 'And I need a young **apprentice**. So come and work for me!' 'OK,' Yukio says happily.

cart a little wooden car that people can pull

clothes people wear these

sorcerer somebody that makes things happen in a way you don't understand

apprentice a young person who works with an older person to learn their job

Yukio goes and says goodbye to Kunio.

That evening, Kunio goes back to his farm and his wife.

But Yukio stays with the sorcerer.

READING CHECK

Match the characters from chapter 3 with the sentences.

Yukio

Mariko

Kunio

a .....Kunio..... wants to sell things from his farm in the nearest town.

b 'Come back soon,' .... says when Kunio and Yukio leave.

c 'Thanks for everything,' .... says to Mariko.

d 'Maybe you can find a job today,' .... tells Yukio on the road.

e .... is interested in everything in the town

f .... is wearing black clothes.

g The sorcerer asks ...., 'Are you looking for work?'

h Yukio says goodbye to .... in the town.

i That evening, Kunio goes back home to ....

j Yukio stays with .... in the town.

The sorcerer

GUESS WHAT

What happens in the next chapter? Tick the boxes.

		Yes	No
a	Yukio goes and lives with the sorcerer.	☐	☐
b	The sorcerer has a little, new house.	☐	☐
c	Yukio works hard in the sorcerer's house.	☐	☐
d	Yukio and the sorcerer get up late every day.	☐	☐
e	The sorcerer stays at home every day.	☐	☐
f	Yukio stays at home every day.	☐	☐
g	The sorcerer reads a big, black book every evening.	☐	☐
h	Yukio soon learns to be a sorcerer.	☐	☐

Chapter 4 At the sorcerer's house

'You must live with me, and work for me now. And you must call me "Grandfather",' the sorcerer says to Yukio. So Yukio goes and lives with the sorcerer in his big, old house.

sweep to move dirty things from the floor

broom a long, thick, wooden stick, with a lot of very thin sticks at one end

Every morning, they get up early. The sorcerer goes out, but Yukio stays at home. He **sweeps** all the rooms in the house with a big **broom**.

It is **winter**, and the days are cold. But there's always a nice, warm **wood fire** in the sorcerer's room.

Every afternoon, Yukio **chops** the wood for the fire with a big **axe**.

Every evening, the sorcerer comes home and eats. He reads for a time. He has a hot **bath** . . .

. . . and then he goes to bed.

winter the coldest time of the year

wood the hard part of a tree

fire this is red and hot, and it burns

chop to make one big thing into many little things with a knife or axe

axe you use this to cut wood

bath when you sit in hot water

For some time, Yukio works hard in the sorcerer's house. But he isn't very happy. 'When can I learn to be a sorcerer?' he asks the old man one evening. 'You must wait,' the sorcerer says to him. 'You're not ready now. When you're ready, you can learn.'

Then the old man reads from a big, black book. Yukio leaves the room, but he listens and watches at the door. He wants to learn **magic** soon. He doesn't want to wait!

magic unusual and making things happen in a way you don't understand

READING CHECK

Correct the mistakes in the sentences.

Grandfather

a Yukio must call the sorcerer ~~'Abe no Seimei'~~.

b The sorcerer lives in a little, old house.

c Every day, Yukio and the sorcerer get up late.

d Yukio never stays at home and works in the house.

e The sorcerer comes home every day in the afternoon.

f The sorcerer eats, writes, has a bath, and goes to bed.

g Yukio wants to learn to be a farmer.

h The sorcerer teaches Yukio magic from his first day at work.

i The sorcerer has a big, red book.

GUESS WHAT

What happens in the next chapter? Tick two boxes to finish each sentence.

a The sorcerer …
  1 ☐ does some magic late at night.
  2 ☐ has a cold bath.
  3 ☐ changes a broom into his helper.
  4 ☐ is angry with Yukio.

b Yukio …
  1 ☐ speaks to the sorcerer.
  2 ☐ watches and listens to the sorcerer.
  3 ☐ reads the big, black book.
  4 ☐ learns something interesting.

Chapter 5

The magic broom

One evening, the sorcerer comes home late. Yukio is in bed. But he isn't sleeping. The door to the old sorcerer's room is open. Yukio can see into it, and hear, too. The sorcerer is reading his big, black, magic book.

Suddenly the old man looks at the broom in the **corner**. He says some magic **words**.

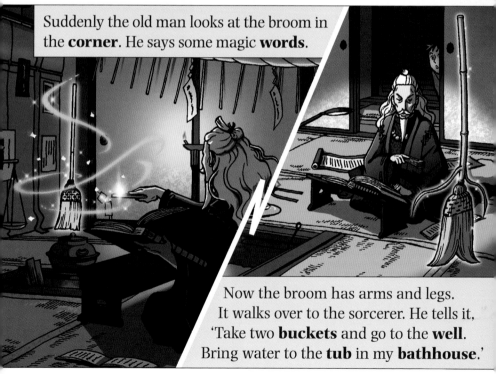

Now the broom has arms and legs. It walks over to the sorcerer. He tells it, 'Take two **buckets** and go to the **well**. Bring water to the **tub** in my **bathhouse**.'

corner where two sides of a room meet

word something we say or write

bucket you can carry water in this

well a place where you can get water from under the ground

tub you can put water in this for a bath, or wash clothes in it

bathhouse a building with a bath or baths in it

16

The broom goes into the garden. Yukio watches it through the window. It takes two buckets to the well. Then it takes water across to the bathhouse again and again.

In the end, the sorcerer goes and speaks to the broom again. He tells it, 'Now make a fire under the tub. I want some nice hot water for my bath.'

So the broom makes a fire under the tub. Soon the water is hot. Then the sorcerer **washes**, and has his bath.

Later, the sorcerer says more magic words. The broom goes into the corner again.

wash to stop your body, or something, from being dirty

It loses its arms and legs, and stops moving. 'Interesting,' Yukio thinks.

READING CHECK

Put the sentences in order. Number them 1–10.

a ☐ The sorcerer speaks to the broom for the last time.

b ☐ The broom suddenly has arms and legs.

c ☐ The sorcerer speaks to the broom for the first time.

d ☐ The sorcerer comes home.

e ☐ The sorcerer has a hot bath.

f ☐ The broom makes a fire under the bath tub.

g ☐ The sorcerer reads his magic book.

h ☐ The broom takes water from the well to the bathhouse.

i ☐ The broom loses its arms and legs.

j ☐ Yukio goes to bed.

GUESS WHAT

What happens in the next chapter? Choose the words to complete the sentences.

a Yukio must wash the sorcerer's *clothes / bird*.

b Yukio does some magic on the *broom / bird*.

c It begins *taking water from the well / hitting Yukio*.

d Yukio *can / can't* stop the broom.

e Suddenly, *the sorcerer / Kunio* arrives.

f He is *nice to / afraid of* Yukio.

Chapter 6

Yukio's spell goes wrong

The next day, the sorcerer leaves the house early. 'It's **laundry** day,' he tells Yukio at the door. 'Put water in the tub in the laundry room. Then wash my clothes.'

After the sorcerer goes, Yukio thinks, 'The broom can help me!' He cannot read. But he remembers the sorcerer's **spell**, and says it.

Suddenly the broom has arms and legs. 'Bring water from the well to the laundry room,' Yukio tells it.

The broom takes water to the laundry room again and again. Soon the laundry tub is **full**. 'Stop!' Yukio cries. But he cannot remember the spell now. So he can't stop the broom!

Yukio chops the broom in two with the axe.

But the two half-brooms change into two new brooms. And they bring more water to the tub.

'Help!' Yukio cries. He chops the two brooms into four ... eight ... sixteen ... thirty-two. Now there are sixty-four. And the laundry room is full of water.

---

aundry when you wash dirty clothes nd make them clean; to do with vashing clothes

spell words that you say to make something happen by magic

full when you can put no more into something; with a lot of something in it

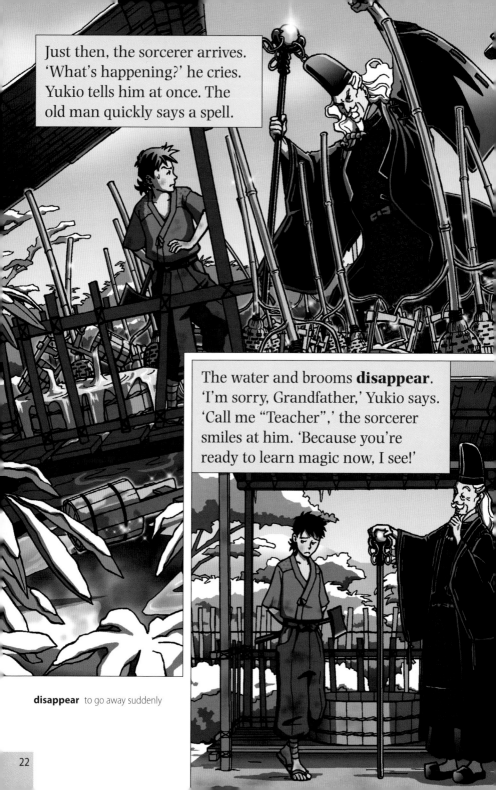

Just then, the sorcerer arrives. 'What's happening?' he cries. Yukio tells him at once. The old man quickly says a spell.

The water and brooms **disappear**. 'I'm sorry, Grandfather,' Yukio says. 'Call me "Teacher",' the sorcerer smiles at him. 'Because you're ready to learn magic now, I see!'

disappear to go away suddenly

READING CHECK

Choose the correct answers.

a What must Yukio do?

1 ☑ the laundry
2 ☐ work in the garden

b Who or what takes the water from the well?

1 ☐ Yukio
2 ☐ the magic broom

c What does Yukio do to the broom?

1 ☐ He chops it in two.
2 ☐ He puts it on the fire.

d Who stops the broom in the end?

1 ☐ Yukio
2 ☐ the sorcerer

e How does the sorcerer feel in the end?

1 ☐ Happy with Yukio.
2 ☐ Angry with Yukio.

GUESS WHAT

What does Yukio do after he learns magic? Choose from these ideas, and write your ideas, too.

a He puts a magic spell on the sorcerer and kills him.

b He goes back to Kunio's farm, and helps Mariko and Kunio.

c He writes a book of magic spells.

d He sells magic to people, and makes a lot of money from this.

e ....

f ....

Project A *Writing a haiku*

A haiku is a Japanese poem. We must count syllables when we write one.
(A syllable is part of a word. There are three syllables in the word 'Jap/an/ese'.)

1 Read the haiku and answer the questions about it.

In the white garden,
I chop firewood and feel hot —
Wood makes us warm twice!

a	How many lines are there?	
b	How many syllables are there in lines 1 and 3?	
c	How many syllables are there in line 2?	
d	What is the time of year? How do we know?	
e	How many /w/ and /f/ sounds can you find?	
f	How can wood make us warm twice?	
g	Which story character is the author of this haiku?	

Sort the lines into a spring and a fall haiku. Which story character is the author of the two poems?

Suddenly birds sing, / A leaf in the fall,
My brother's leaving home now / And trees wear lovely blossoms
And I must stay here. / When my love arrives.

Spring Haiku

....
....
....

Fall Haiku

....
....
....

by: ....

Choose a new story character and time of the year. Write a haiku about that season by your character.

Project B *Different versions of a story*

1 Read about another version of *The Sorcerer's Apprentice*. Which parts are different from the story in this book? Underline them.

The Sorcerer's Apprentice is a 1797 poem by the German writer Goethe (1749–1832). The story happens in Brandenburg. The poem is 407 words long and has 14 verses. In this version of the story, the apprentice has no name, no sister, and no brother-in-law. The poem begins after the sorcerer leaves home. Then the apprentice remembers and says the sorcerer's spell to give arms and legs and a head to a broom. He puts an old coat on the broom, too. He asks the broom for water for his bath. The broom brings the water from the river. Soon the bath is full. But the apprentice forgets the spell to take away the magic from the broom. So he chops the broom in two with an axe. Now two brooms bring water to the bath. The apprentice calls for help from his master. The poem ends when the sorcerer comes back and stops the magic with a spell. He tells the broom, 'Spirits must only come when a true master calls.'

Goethe

2 Write a short text about the story in this book. Use the text in activity 1 to help you.

....

....

....

....

....

....

....

....

....

....

....

....

....

....

....

3 Use the Internet to find out more about one of these versions of the story. Write a short text about it.

The Sorcerer's Apprentice
live-action feature movie (2005)

The Sorcerer's Apprentice
short cartoon movie (1940)

The Lover of Lies
story by Lucian (AD 150)

WORD WORK 1

1 These words don't match the pictures. Correct them.

a ~~parents~~
...........jobs...........

b cherries

c blossoms

d fireflies

e birds

f jobs

2 Complete the sentences with other new words from Chapters 1 and 2 in the correct form.

a 'Can you help me?' ' M a y b e I can. What's wrong?'

b His mother and father are very happy _ o _ e _ _ e _ .

c I like the _ _ _ i _ _ – when our garden has new flowers in it.

d Her brother has a big, old _ a _ _ in the country.

e She works very _ a _ _ at the office from Monday to Friday.

f Would you like your _ e _ with or without milk?

g Next _ u _ _ e _ we're going to visit friends in Turkey.

h Miranda is _ a _ _ _ i _ _ Paul on June 25th this year.

i This is my friend Ed, and that's Ed's _ i _ e, Pam, over there.

WORD WORK 2

Find words from Chapters 3 and 4 to match the pictures.

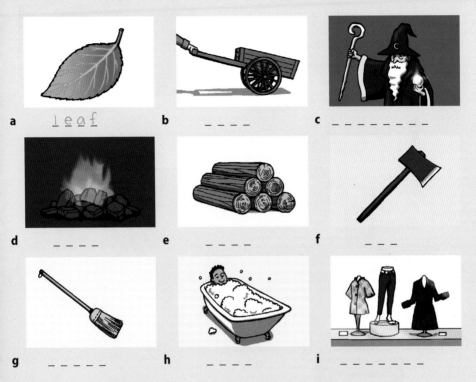

a l e a f

b _ _ _ _

c _ _ _ _ _ _ _ _

d _ _ _ _

e _ _ _ _

f _ _ _

g _ _ _ _ _

h _ _ _ _

i _ _ _ _ _ _ _

2 Complete each sentence with a word from the box.

> ~~apprentice~~ chop fall magic sell sweep winter

a The interesting old man is looking for an …apprentice… .

b The …………………, when the trees go red, is a beautiful time of the year.

c Kunio wants to …………………things from his farm in town.

d Can you …………………under the table? It's very dirty there.

e Yukio wants to learn some …………………from the sorcerer soon.

f I can …………………the apple for your bird.

g In Australia, June, July, and August are in the ………………… .

WORD WORK 3

1 Find words in the books to match the pictures.

lelw

recnor

a ....well................. **b** ....

tucbek

teshuhoba

c .... **d** ....

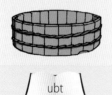

ubt

e ....

2 Correct each underlined word with a new word from Chapters 5 and 6.

a I can't eat any more. I'm <u>feel</u>. ....full.........

b *Karate* and *judo* are Japanese <u>works</u>. ....

c When Yukio says the magic <u>speak</u> the broom begins to help him. ....

d When he says 'Abracadabra', the birds suddenly <u>different</u>. ....

e All your clothes are dirty. You need to do your <u>laughing</u>. ....

GRAMMAR CHECK

Present Simple: third person –s

We add –s to the infinitive without *to* to make the third person (he / she / it) form of the Present Simple.

Yukio lives in old Japan.

When verbs end in o, ch, ss, sh, we add –es to make the third person form. When verbs end in consonant + y, we change the y to i and add –es.

The sorcerer goes out in the morning.

'Help!' Yukio cries.

The verbs be and have have irregular third person –s forms in the Present Simple.

The sorcerer is very interesting.

He has a big, old house.

We can use the Present Simple to tell a story.

Complete these sentences with the verbs in brackets in the Present Simple.

a Kunio . . . . . . *lives* . . . . . . (live) in the country.

b He . . . . (have) a farm near Mariko's house.

c He . . . . (finish) work early.

d He . . . . (walk) past Mariko's garden.

e He . . . . (watch) Mariko when she is working.

f He . . . . (love) her a lot.

g Mariko . . . . (be) interested in Kunio.

h She . . . . (marry) him in the summer.

i She . . . . (go) and lives on Kunio's farm.

j She . . . . (take) her brother with her.

k She . . . . (wash) Kunio's clothes for him.

l She . . . . (cry) after her brother leaves home.

GRAMMAR

Imperatives

We make the imperative using the infinitive without *to*.

Have some tea!   *Look at those fireflies!*

We put don't before the verb to make the negative imperative.

Don't marry Kunio!   *Don't be angry with me!*

2 Complete the sentences with the imperative form of the verbs in the box.

be   come   not forget   not sleep   ~~smile~~   talk

a '.......Smile........ at Kunio!' Mariko tells Yukio.

b '........................ with me!' Mariko says to her brother.

c '........................ under that tree!' Kunio tells Yukio.

d '........................ to me!' Yukio says to the birds.

e '........................ nice to Yukio!' Mariko says to Kunio.

f '........................ – he's my little brother,' she tells him.

3 What does the sorcerer tell Yukio? Complete his words.

bring   chop   ~~get up~~   make   not do   not leave
not read   put   remember   sweep   wash

a) ....Get up........! It's late. **b)** .... my breakfast to me. Then

c) .... some wood and **d)** .... a fire in my room.

e) .... my magic book, and **f)** .... the house at all.

g) .... all the rooms with the broom. **h)** ....

some water in the laundry tub; and **i)** .... my clothes for me.

And **j)** .... – **k)** .... any magic!

GRAMMAR CHECK

Adjectives and adverbs of manner

We use adjectives to describe people or things. They tell us more about <u>nouns</u>.

Yukio is angry.   *The cherry tree is beautiful.*

We use adverbs of manner to talk about how we do things. They tell us more about <u>verbs</u>.

Yukio <u>speaks</u> to Kunio angrily.

Mariko <u>moves</u> beautifully.

To make regular adverbs, we add –ly to the adjective.

beautiful – beautifully

Adjectives that end in –y, we change to –ily.

angry – angrily

Some adverbs are irregular.

Yukio drinks his tea fast. (adjective = fast)

Kunio works hard on the farm. (adjective = hard)

The sorcerer comes home late. (adjective = late)

Circle the correct word to complete each sentence.

a Yukio's mother and father are *dead* / *deadly*.

b Mariko works *hardly* / *hard* in the house and garden.

c Kunio and Mariko laugh *happily* / *happy* together.

d Yukio is *interested* / *interestedly* in everything in the town.

e Yukio goes after the sorcerer *excitedly* / *excited*.

f Kunio arrives at the farm *late* / *lately* that night.

g Yukio says the magic words *careful* / *carefully*.

h The broom goes to and from the well very *fast* / *fastly*.

i Soon the tub is *full* / *fully* of water.

j *Sudden* / *Suddenly*, the sorcerer arrives.

k He says a *quick* / *quickly* spell and stops the magic.

DOMINOES THE STRUCTURED APPROACH TO READING IN ENGLISH

Dominoes is an enjoyable series of illustrated classic and modern stories in four carefully graded language stages – from Starter to Three – which take learners from beginner to intermediate level.

Each *Domino* reader includes:
- a good story to read and enjoy
- integrated activities to develop reading skills and increase active vocabulary
- personalized projects to make the language and story themes more meaningful
- contextualized grammar practice.

Each *Domino* pack contains a reader, plus a MultiROM with:
- a complete audio recording of the story, fully dramatized to bring it to life
- interactive activities to offer further practice in reading and language skills and to consolidate learning.

If you liked this Quick Starter Level *Domino*, why not read these?

Ali Baba and the Forty Thieves
Retold by Janet Hardy-Gould

Ali Baba finds a thieves' treasure cave and he is suddenly rich. Then his brother Kasim visits the cave, and things go wrong. The forty thieves find Kasim there, kill him, and cut his body into four pieces. What can Ali Baba do? He wants to bury his brother quietly, but how can he? Morgiana, his servant-girl, has the answer. But what can she do when the thieves find Ali Baba and want to kill him, too?

Book ISBN: 978 0 19 424934 8
MultiROM Pack ISBN: 978 0 19 424932 4

Troy
Bill Bowler

'I see Troy in flames years from now – because Paris brings disaster to us,' says Queen Hecuba about her son.

Paris's father, King Priam, wants to kill him. But Paris lives, and later loves Helen – King Menelaus's queen – from Greece. When Paris brings Helen to Troy, war begins between the Trojans and Greeks.

What happens when Paris's brother Hector, and the Greek fighter Achilles, meet in battle? Who wins the war, and how? Read *Troy* and find the answers.

Book ISBN: 978 0 19 424970 6
MultiROM Pack ISBN: 978 0 19 424954 6

You can find details and a full list of books in the Oxford Graded Readers catalogue and Oxford English Language Teaching Catalogue, and on the website: www.oup.com/elt

Teachers: see www.oup.com/elt for a full range of online support, or consult your local office.

	CEFR	Cambridge Exams	IELTS	TOEFL iBT	TOEIC
Level 3	B1	PET	4.0	57–86	550
Level 2	A2–B1	KET-PET	3.0-4.0	–	–
Level 1	A1–A2	YLE Flyers/KET	3.0	–	–
Starter & Quick Starter	A1	YLE Movers	–	–	–